Pebble® Plus

ICE AGE ANIMALS

Arctic Shrews

by Joy Frisch-Schmoll

Consulting Editor: Gail Saunders-Smith, PhD

Content Consultant: Margaret M. Yacobucci, PhD
Education and Outreach Coordinator,
Paleontological Society; Associate Professor,
Department of Geology, Bowling Green State University

CAPSTONE PRESS
a capstone imprint

Pebble Plus is published by Capstone Press,
1710 Roe Crest Drive, North Mankato, Minnesota 56003
www.capstonepub.com

Library of Congress Cataloging-in-Publication Data
Frisch-Schmoll, Joy, author.
Arctic Shrews / by Joy Frisch-Schmoll.
pages cm.—(Pebble Plus. Ice Age Animals)
Summary: "Describes the characteristics, food, habitat, behavior, life
cycle, and threats to arctic shrews"—Provided by publisher.
Audience: Ages 5-7.
Audience: K to grade 3.
Includes bibliographical references and index.
ISBN 978-1-4914-2099-7 (library binding)
ISBN 978-1-4914-2317-2 (pbk.)
ISBN 978-1-4914-2340-0 (ebook pdf)
1. Shrews—Canada—Juvenile literature. 2. Shrews—North
America—Juvenile literature. I. Title.
QL737.S75F75 2015
599.33′6—dc23   2014028915

Editorial Credits
Jeni Wittrock, editor; Peggie Carley and Janet Kusmierski, designers;
Wanda Winch, media researcher; Laura Manthe, production specialist

Photo Credits
Illustrator: Jon Hughes
Shutterstock: Alex Staroseltsev, snowball, April Cat, icicles, Leigh Prather,
ice crystals, LilKar, cover background, pcruciatti, interior background

Note to Parents and Teachers

The Ice Age Animals set supports national science standards related to life science.
This book describes and illustrates arctic shrews. The images support early readers in
understanding the text. The repetition of words and phrases helps early readers learn
new words. This book also introduces early readers to subject-specific vocabulary words,
which are defined in the Glossary section. Early readers may need assistance to read
some words and to use the Table of Contents, Glossary, Read More, Internet Sites, and
Index sections of the book.

Printed in China by Nordica.
0914/CA21401504
092014   008470NORDS15

Table of Contents

Small Survivor

A tiny creature darts through the weeds. It spies a grasshopper and—pounce! It catches the insect and eats it. Then the furry hunter hurries on.

Shrew Bodies

An arctic shrew is one of

the world's smallest mammals.

A shrew has a long tail

and a pointed snout.

Its eyes and ears are tiny.

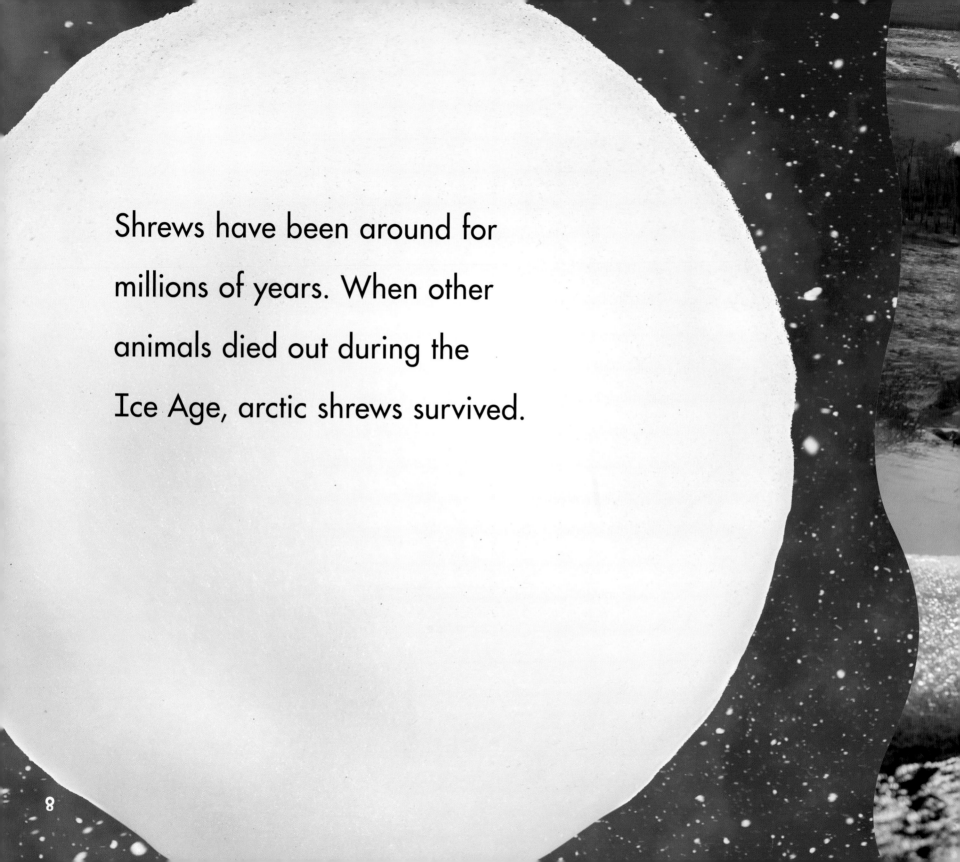

Shrews have been around for millions of years. When other animals died out during the Ice Age, arctic shrews survived.

9

Grassy Home

Today arctic shrews live in Canada and the northern United States. They like grassy wetlands such as marshes and swamps.

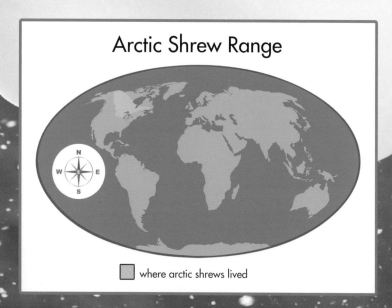

Arctic Shrew Range

where arctic shrews lived

Arctic shrews build their homes
in old stumps and under logs
and rocks. Their nests are
made of dried grass, leaves,
and moss.

Time to Eat

Shrews are always hungry. They must eat every few hours to stay alive. Hunting day and night, they search for insects, snails, and worms.

Sniff! Shrews find bugs
with their noses. They catch
bugs with their sharp teeth.
Shrews can eat their own
weight in food every day!

A Short Life

A female shrew usually has two litters a year. She gives birth to four to nine babies. The babies are born blind and naked.

When young shrews can care
for themselves, they live alone.
They don't like to be around
other shrews. Shrews live
up to 18 months.

Glossary

Ice Age—a time when Earth was covered in ice; the last ice age ended about 11,500 years ago

litter—a group of animals born at the same time to the same mother

mammal—a warm-blooded animal that breathes air; mammals have hair or fur; female mammals feed milk to their young

marsh—an area of low, wet land

snout—the long front part of an animal's head; it includes the nose, mouth, and jaws

swamp—an area with trees that is partly covered by water

Read More

Lister, Adrian. *The Ice Age Tracker's Guide.* London: Frances Lincoln Children's Books, 2010.

Tait, Leia. *Mice.* New York: Weigl Publishers Inc., 2010.

Weiss, Ellen. *The Taming of Lola: A Shrew Story.* New York: Abrams Books for Young Readers, 2010.

Internet Sites

FactHound offers a safe, fun way to find Internet sites related to this book. All of the sites on FactHound have been researched by our staff.

Here's all you do:

Visit *www.facthound.com*

Type in this code: 9781491420997

 Check out projects, games and lots more at **www.capstonekids.com**

Index

Word Count: 211

Grade: 1

Early-Intervention Level: 17